Getting Sick
and
Feeling Better

Carron Brown and Wesley Robins

Kane Miller
A DIVISION OF EDC PUBLISHING

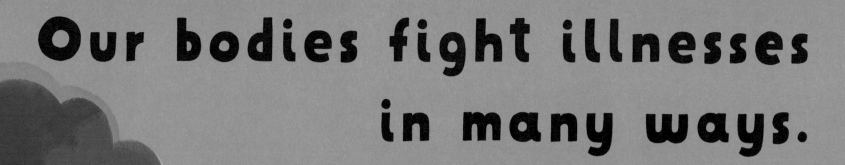

Our bodies fight illnesses in many ways.

There are lots of things we can do to help ourselves get better.

Shine a flashlight behind the page or hold it to the light to reveal what happens when we get sick. Discover a hidden world of great surprises.

George isn't feeling well. He's very warm, and his skin feels hot to the touch.

What's under his arm?

A thermometer.
It measures the temperature
inside the body.

The thermometer shows
that George has a fever.

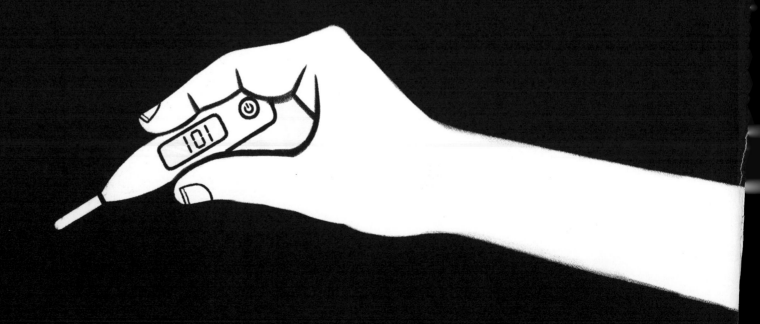

Aaah-choo!

Ellie has a cold.

What's making
her sneeze?

Gooey mucus is inside her nose. The body creates mucus to trap germs when it's fighting a cold. Germs are tiny things that can make people sick.

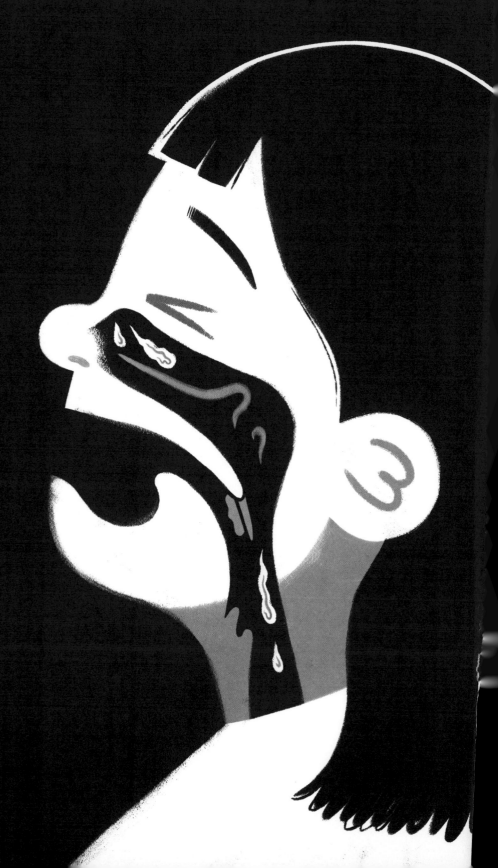

Ben is blowing his nose to unblock mucus so that he can breathe more easily.

What should he do with the tissue now?

Used tissues go in the trash.

This helps to protect other people from catching germs and getting sick.

Meera has a tickly throat and is coughing.

What happens when she coughs?

Coughing is another way
that the body gets rid of
mucus, and the germs that
have been trapped.

George is opening the door to the bathroom.

What has he left on the handle?

Germs! The germs
are too tiny to see,
but they are there.

If other people
touch the germs,
then they might
get sick, too.

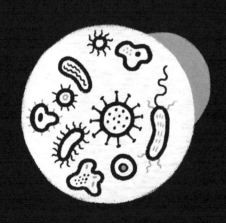

Ellie is at the sink. What's she doing?

She's washing her hands
with soap and warm water.

Cleaning her hands means that germs
won't be left on things that she touches.

Ben is getting a spoonful of medicine. Sometimes, our bodies need medicine to help fight sickness.

Where is the medicine bottle?

It's in the
refrigerator.

Some medicines
need to be kept cool.

The curtains are closed, even though it's daytime.

Who's under the covers?

It's Meera! She's getting lots of rest.

Sleeping helps our bodies heal.

Glug! Glug!

George is thirsty.

What's he drinking?

It's water. George's body has used lots of water through sweating and making mucus.

We need to drink water all of the time, but especially when we're sick.

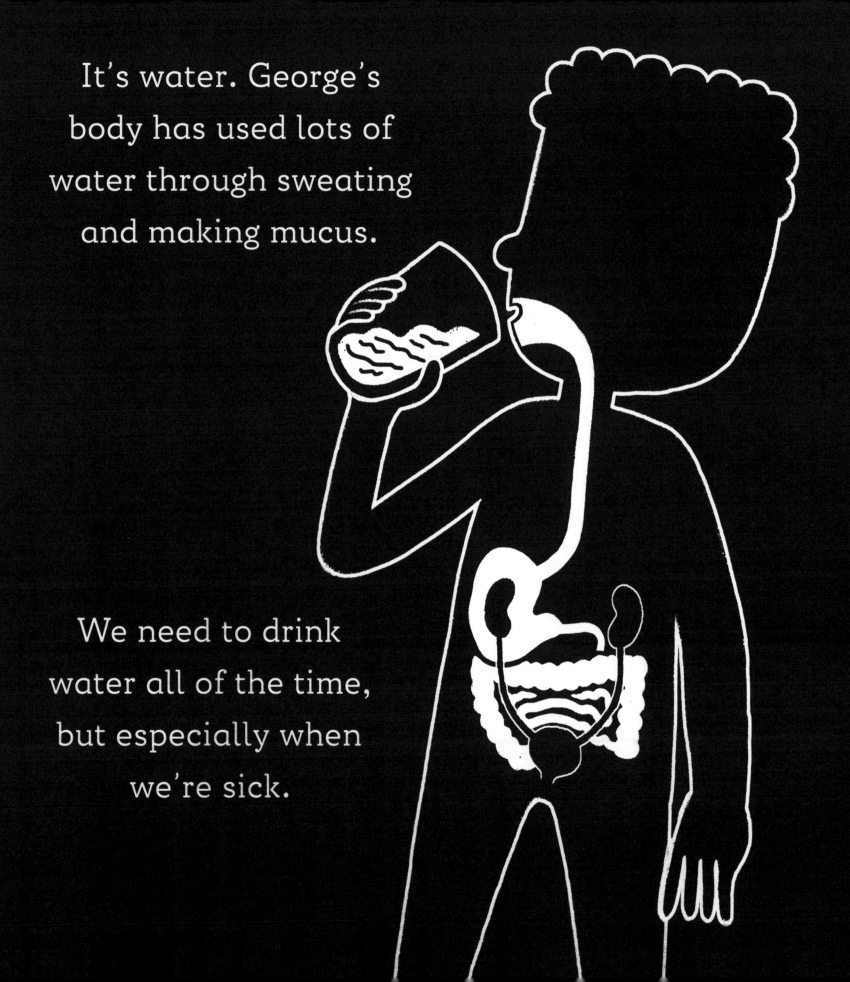

Yum! This snack is really tasty.

What's in Ellie's bowl?

It's a fruit salad.

Eating lots of healthy foods
keeps our bodies fit and strong.
And they taste good, too!

Ben is feeling well enough
to go outside. It's a beautiful day,
and the sun is shining.

What does sunlight
help with?

Our bones!

Sunlight gives our
bodies vitamin D,
which helps keep
our bones and
teeth healthy.

It's good to be in the fresh air.

What's Meera doing now?

She's jumping on a trampoline
and feeling much better!

Whoosh!

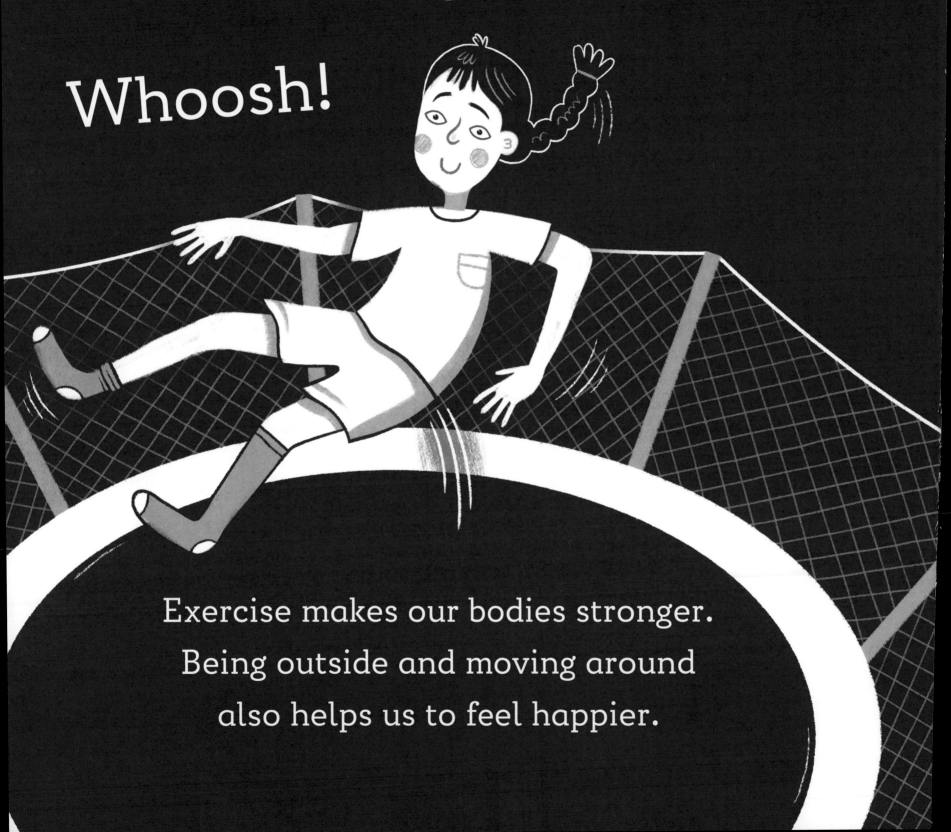

Exercise makes our bodies stronger.
Being outside and moving around
also helps us to feel happier.

It's the evening. George is using the computer.

Who's on the screen?

"Hello!" George is talking
to his grandma.

Grandma has stayed at home while George has been
ill, to keep from getting sick, too. She'll visit soon,
now that he's free of germs and feeling better.

Ellie's uncle has also caught a cold.
He can't go to the store right now.

What's in
the bags?

The bags are full of delicious and
healthy food for him to eat.

Sometimes when people are sick,
they need a helping hand.

Ben sees a person
wearing a face mask.

What's under
the mask?

A smile!

Often people wear masks to keep themselves and others safe from germs.

Everyone is at the park, having fun.

It feels so good to be well!

There's more...

The body does a lot to keep a person well. Read more about the signs of sickness and what you can do to prevent it.

Fever

A healthy body temperature is 97°F to 99°F. The body raises its temperature to slow down sickness and fight germs.

Sneezing

Sneezing is the body's way of cleaning the nose of germs. Use a tissue when sneezing to catch the germs and wash your hands afterward.

Coughing

Mucus running down the back of the throat can make it tickle. When coughing, use a tissue to catch the germs, and wash your hands afterward.

Germs

Germs are very tiny bacteria and viruses that make people sick. They can spread when sick people cough or sneeze. Washing our hands helps to kill germs and stop them from spreading.

Medicine

Medicine can help sick people feel better. There are many kinds of medicine. Sometimes, a visit to a doctor is needed to find out which medicine is best to take.

Sleeping

Resting boosts the body's fight against illness and gives it time to heal. Feeling tired is the body's way of saying "slow down."

Vitamins

We need vitamins to help us grow and stay well. Most vitamins are taken in by the body through eating food, such as vegetables and fruits, but vitamin D can come from sunlight.

Face Mask

A mask worn over the nose and mouth can help stop germs in the air from being breathed into the body. If a person is sick, they might wear a mask to stop spreading germs to others.

Exercise

Getting up and moving helps bones and muscles stay strong. Exercising also releases chemicals called endorphins ("en-door-fins") that make a person feel good.

First American Edition 2022
Kane Miller, A Division of EDC Publishing

Copyright © 2022 Quarto Publishing plc

For information contact:
Kane Miller, A Division of EDC Publishing
5402 S 122nd E Ave
Tulsa, OK 74146
www.kanemiller.com
www.myubam.com

Library of Congress Control Number: 2021937033

Printed in Shenzhen, China. PP1021

ISBN: 978-1-68464-282-3

1 2 3 4 5 6 7 8 9 10

MIX
Paper from
responsible sources
FSC® C001701
FSC
www.fsc.org